OFFICIAL

Pokémon

Pokédex

®

Normal

OFFICIAL

POKéMON

Pokédex

Psychic

By Tracey West
and Katherine Noll

SCHOLASTIC INC.

New York   Toronto   London   Auckland   Sydney
Mexico City   New Delhi   Hong Kong   Buenos Aires

ISBN 0-439-85586-1

12 11 10 9 8 7 6 5 4 3   6 7 8/ 0

Printed in the U.S.A.
First printing, January 2006

Contents

Words

In this book you will find a few special Pokémon terms. Here is a list to help you on your journey:

✳ **Moves**: Each Pokémon has special skills that it uses in battle. Different Pokémon know different moves.

✳ **Evolves**: When a Pokémon evolves, it changes into a new form. **Chansey** evolves into **Blissey**. This book will tell you when or if this can happen to a Pokémon. Evolutions are shown using arrows.

✳ **Type**: Each Pokémon is identified with a Type. Some Types are Fire, Water, and Normal. The Type of Pokémon you have determines what kinds of Pokémon yours will be strong against in battle. A Pokémon can also be more than one Type. **Hoothoot** is both a Normal and a Flying Pokémon.

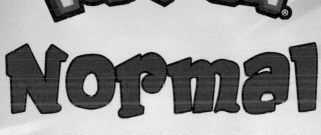

What's Inside . . .

This Pokédex tells you everything you need to know about Normal Pokémon, from Aipom to Zigzagoon. Here you will find:

* ✵ Stats for 50 Normal Pokémon.
* ✵ A chart of 13 Normal/Flying Types.
* ✵ An inside look at the Petalburg City Gym.
* ✵ A talk with Meowth.

So prepare yourself for the not-so-normal world of Normal Type Pokémon. Who knows? After you finish this book, you may become a Master of Normal Pokémon!

Normal Pokémon?
Think Again!

You might think there's nothing special about Normal Pokémon. You might think they are boring compared to Fire Types or Electric Types. You might even think that Normal Pokémon can't help you in battle.

If you think these things, you are wrong! Don't let their name fool you! Normal Type Pokémon are very special. Kecleon can change color to blend in with things around it. Blissey can make people happy. Castform can make itself look like the weather. Not bad for a couple of Normal Pokémon! And their attacks can catch your opponent off guard. Lots of Normal Pokémon look strange, too.

Take Lickitung—there's nothing normal about its long, sticky tongue!

So get ready for some surprises when you read about the world of Normal Pokémon. You are in for a very strange and unusual time!

Battle Tips
for Normal Types

One of the things a Pokémon Trainer needs to know is which Pokémon to choose in a battle. If you battle with a Normal Pokémon, here are some things to keep in mind:

Normal Pokémon will do the least damage to Rock Pokémon—such as Sudowoodo—or to Steel Pokémon—such as Registeel. If your opponent uses either one of these Types, keep your Normal Pokémon in its ball!

When Normal Pokémon fight Ghost Pokémon, such as Dusclops, the attacks of Normal Pokémon do no damage. So you should use a Type other than Normal

As for all of the other Types—anything can happen! So grab your Normal Pokémon and start battling!

Cute **Cleffa** is shaped like a little star. When there are a lot of shooting stars in the sky, large groups of **Cleffa** will gather together and dance. **Clefairy** can be hard to find. But it's easier to spot one on the night of the full moon! And if you are lucky enough to catch one, you can evolve it into the rare **Clefable**. But first, you will need a Moon Stone.

Cleffa
Star Shape Pokémon

Pronunciation:
CLEH-fuh

Possible Moves:
Pound, Charm, Encore, Sing, Sweet Kiss, Magical Leaf

Evolves: with Friendship

Clefairy
Fairy Pokémon

Pronunciation:
cluh-FAIR-ee

Possible Moves:
Pound, Growl, Encore, Sing, Doubleslap, Follow Me, Minimize, Defense Curl, Metronome, Light Screen, Cosmic Power, Moonlight, Meteor Mash

Evolves: with a Moon Stone

Clefable
Fairy Pokémon

Pronunciation:
cluh-FAY-bull

Possible Moves:
Sing, Doubleslap, Minimize, Metronome

Does not evolve

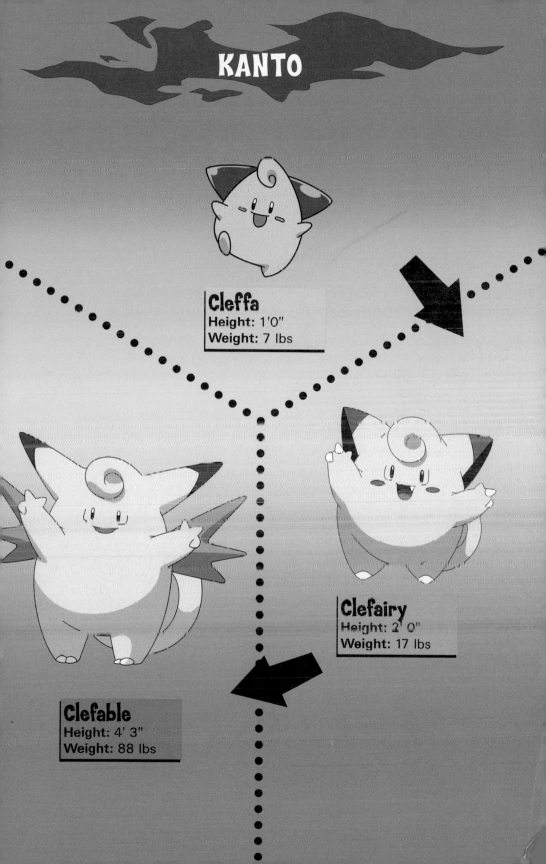

KANTO

Cleffa
Height: 1'0"
Weight: 7 lbs

Clefairy
Height: 2' 0"
Weight: 17 lbs

Clefable
Height: 4' 3"
Weight: 88 lbs

And the best Pokémon Parent Award goes to—**Kangaskhan**! This Normal Pokémon carries its baby in a special stomach pouch. **Kangaskhan** will do anything to keep its baby safe. The baby **Kangaskhan** lives in the pouch until it's about three years old. If you see a young **Kangaskhan** playing by itself, don't try to catch it. You may find an angry adult **Kangaskhan** charging at you ready to protect its young!

Kangaskhan
Parent Pokémon

Pronunciation:
KANG-guhs-con

Possible Moves:
Comet Punch, Leer, Bite, Tail Whip, Fake Out, Mega Punch, Rage, Endure, Dizzy Punch, Reversal

Does not evolve

Kangaskhan
Height: 7' 3"
Weight: 176 lbs

Munchlax is one hungry little Pokémon. It loves to eat so much that it will steal food to fill its hungry belly! When **Munchlax** evolves into **Snorlax**, it gets even hungrier. **Snorlax** is so lazy! It just eats and sleeps all day. And **Snorlax** is very mellow. In fact, it lets little children play on its big belly when it sleeps.

Munchlax
Big Eater Pokémon

Pronunciation:
MUNCH-lacks

Height: 2' 0"
Weight: 232 lbs

Possible Moves:
unknown

Evolves: unknown

Snorlax
Sleeping Pokémon

Pronunciation:
SNORE-lacks

Height: 6' 11"
Weight: 1,014 lbs

Possible Moves:
Tackle, Amnesia, Defense Curl, Belly Drum, Covet, Headbutt, Yawn, Rest, Snore, Body Slam, Sleep Talk, Block, Rollout, Hyper Beam

Does not evolve

It's hard to walk around and not bump into a **Rattata**. This common Pokémon has very sharp teeth and eats anything. If you think a **Rattata** has sharp teeth, check out **Raticate**'s chompers! Its fangs never stop growing. **Raticate**'s fangs are so sharp that it can topple a concrete building just by gnawing on it!

Raticate
Mouse Pokémon

Pronunciation: RAT-ih-kit

Height: 2' 4"
Weight: 41 lbs

Possible Moves: Tackle, Tail Whip, Quick Attack, Hyper Fang, Scary Face, Pursuit, Super Fang, Endeavor

Does not evolve

Rattata
Mouse Pokémon

Pronunciation: rah-TA-tah

Height: 1' 0"
Weight: 8 lbs

Possible Moves: Tackle, Tail Whip, Quick Attack, Hyper Fang, Focus Energy, Pursuit, Super Fang, Endeavor

Evolves: at level 20

Both **Meowth** and **Persian** have an attack that greedy people love. Pay Day gives its Trainer extra money after each win! **Meowth** loves sparkling coins and jewels. Maybe that's why a **Meowth** is part of Team Rocket—**Meowth** is a natural thief!

Team Rocket's Boss has a pet **Persian**. It's beautiful but mean! If you try to pet a **Persian**, it might scratch you for no reason.

Persian
Classy Cat Pokémon

Pronunciation:
PURR-zhin

Height: 3' 3"
Weight: 71 lbs

Possible Moves:
Scratch, Growl, Bite,
Pay Day, Faint Attack,
Screech, Fury Swipes,
Slash, Fake Out,
Swagger

Does not evolve

Meowth
Scratch Cat Pokémon

Pronunciation:
mee-OWTH

Height: 1' 4"
Weight: 9 lbs

Possible Moves:
Scratch, Growl, Bite,
Pay Day, Faint Attack,
Screech, Fury Swipes,
Slash, Fake Out,
Swagger

Evolves: at level 28

Lickitung looks like a champion lollipop licker! Almost seven feet long and covered with thick, gooey saliva, **Lickitung's** tongue can stick to anything. In a battle, its tongue is tough to beat! With one lick, **Lickitung's** enemies will feel a tingling sensation that can cause paralysis. If you don't like being slobbered on, **Lickitung** is *not* the Pokémon for you!

Lickitung
Licking Pokémon

Pronunciation:
LICK-ih-tung

Possible Moves:
Lick, Supersonic, Defense Curl, Knock Off, Stomp, Wrap, Disable, Slam, Screech, Refresh

Does not evolve

Lickitung
Height: 3' 11"
Weight: 144 lbs

KANTO & JOHTO

You are more likely to find **Chansey** in a Pokémon Center than out in the wild. These kind Pokémon are natural-born nurses. **Chansey** will share their delicious and nutritious eggs with any injured Pokémon that needs help.

Blissey also cares for sick Pokémon. Just one bite of **Blissey's** egg will make you happy. If you are feeling sad, **Blissey** can sense it with its fluffy coat of fur. It will quickly offer you an egg!

Blissey
Happiness Pokémon

Pronunciation:
BLIH-see

Height: 4' 11"
Weight: 103 lbs

Possible Moves:
Pound, Growl, Tail Whip, Refresh, Softboiled, Sing, Doubleslap, Minimize, Egg Bomb, Defense Curl, Light Screen, Double-Edge

Does not evolve

Chansey
Egg Pokémon

Pronunciation:
CHAN-see

Height: 3' 7"
Weight: 76 lbs

Possible Moves:
Pound, Growl, Tail Whip, Refresh, Softboiled, Sing, Doubleslap, Minimize, Egg Bomb, Defense Curl, Light Screen, Double-Edge

Evolves: with Friendship

Did somebody say bullheaded? That's a perfect description of **Tauros**. These Normal Pokémon are stubborn—and very tough. **Tauros** live in herds. The bull-like Pokémon fight each other to prove their strength.

Watch out if you see **Tauros** whipping itself with its three tails. That means it's getting ready to charge—and fight!

Tauros
Wild Bull Pokémon

Pronunciation:
TOR-ohs

Possible Moves:
Tackle, Tail Whip, Rage, Horn Attack, Scary Face, Pursuit, Swagger, Rest, Thrash, Take Down

Does not evolve

Tauros
Height: 4' 7"
Weight: 195 lbs

Are you seeing double? Maybe there's a **Ditto** around! **Ditto** can transform into any Pokémon. **Ditto** will copy its opponent's DNA to make a perfect double.

Not sure if the Pokémon you are battling is the real thing? Make it laugh. **Ditto** can't keep up its disguise while it's laughing!

Ditto
Transform Pokémon

Pronunciation:
DID-oh

Height: 1' 0"
Weight: 9 lbs

Possible Moves:
Transform

Does not evolve

Tip:
Want to make your **Ditto's** defense stronger? Use an item called **Metal Powder**.

Eevee evolves into five different Pokémon. If exposed to Element Stones, **Eevee's** DNA will change and **Eevee** evolves.

Umbreon
(Dark Type)

Espeon
(Psychic Type)

with Friendship during the day

with Friendship at night

Flareon
(Fire Type)

with a Fire Stone

with a Water Stone

Vaporeon
(Water Type)

with a Thunder Stone

Jolteon
(Electric Type)

Eevee
Evolution Pokémon

Pronunciation:
EE-vee

Height: 1' 0"
Weight: 14 lbs

Possible Moves:
Tackle, Tail Whip, Helping Hand, Sand-Attack, Growl, Quick Attack, Bite, Baton Pass, Take Down

Would you like to have a pet you don't have to walk? Then **Porygon** is perfect for you! This virtual Pokémon was created on a computer. **Porygon** can travel freely in cyberspace. The upgraded version, **Porygon2**, can learn new things on its own. Since both **Porygon** and **Porygon2** don't breathe, they are being considered for space exploration.

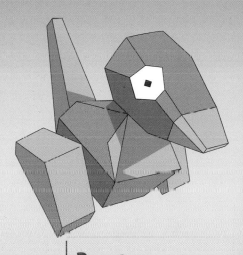

Porygon 2
Virtual Pokémon

Pronunciation:
POR-eh-gon TOO

Height: 2' 0"
Weight: 72 lbs

Possible Moves:
Tackle, Conversion, Conversion 2, Agility, Psybeam, Recover, Defense Curl, Lock-On, Tri Attack, Recycle, Zap Cannon

Does not evolve

Porygon
Virtual Pokémon

Pronunciation:
POR-eh-gon

Height: 2' 7"
Weight: 80 lbs

Possible Moves:
Tackle, Conversion, Conversion 2, Agility, Psybeam, Recover, Sharpen, Lock-On, Tri Attack, Recycle, Zap Cannon

Evolves: with a Trade

Who needs a burglar alarm with **Sentret** around? If there's danger, this Pokémon will let you know! **Sentret** stands on the tip of its tail to look around. If it spots an enemy, it lets out a loud cry and hits the ground with its tail. When **Sentret** evolves into **Furret**, it stays safe by living deep in the ground. Only **Furret**'s long, narrow body can fit inside its mazelike burrows!

Sentret
Scout Pokémon

Pronunciation:
SEN-trit

Height: 2' 7"
Weight: 13 lbs

Possible Moves:
Scratch, Defense Curl, Quick Attack, Fury Swipes, Helping Hand, Slam, Follow Me, Rest, Amnesia

Evolves: at level 15

Furret
Long Body Pokémon

Pronunciation:
FUR-eht

Height: 5' 11"
Weight: 72 lbs

Possible Moves:
Scratch, Defense Curl, Quick Attack, Fury Swipes, Helping Hand, Slam, Follow Me, Rest, Amnesia

Does not evolve

Everyone remembers Misty's adorable **Togepi**. If you are lucky enough to catch one of your own, you are going to be the happiest Trainer around! **Togepi** stores up happiness inside its shell and then shares it with others. Make sure you treat your **Togepi** nicely. That's how it will evolve into **Togetic**! The flying **Togetic** will appear to caring people, showering them with happiness.

Togetic
Happiness Pokémon

Pronunciation:
TOE-guh-tick

Height: 2' 0"
Weight: 7 lbs

Possible Moves:
Magical Leaf, Growl,
Charm, Metronome,
Yawn, Sweet Kiss,
Encore, Wish,
Ancientpower,
Follow Me, Safeguard,
Double-Edge,
Baton Pass

Does not evolve

Togepi
Spike Ball Pokémon

Pronunciation:
TOE-guh-pee

Height: 1' 0"
Weight: 3 lbs

Possible Moves:
Growl, Charm,
Wish, Metronome,
Sweet Kiss, Yawn,
Encore, Follow Me,
Ancientpower, Safeguard,
Double-Edge, Baton Pass

Evolves: with Friendship

Dual Type:
Normal/Flying

If you try to catch a **Dunsparce**, it will use its tail to get away from you! **Dunsparce** has a drill for a tail, which it uses to burrow into the ground and escape. **Dunsparce** makes its nests deep in the ground. Did you notice **Dunsparce**'s tiny wings? **Dunsparce** can't fly, but it can float in the air using its wings.

Dunsparce
Land Snake Pokémon

Pronunciation:
DUHN-sparce

Possible Moves:
Rage, Defense Curl, Yawn, Glare, Rollout, Spite, Pursuit, Screech, Take Down, Flail, Endeavor

Does not evolve

Dunsparce
Height: 4' 11"
Weight: 31 lbs

Do you love cute Pokémon but like fierce ones, too? If so, then catch a **Teddiursa**. You can play with the adorable little teddy bear, and then evolve it into a big bad **Ursaring**!

Teddiursa's favorite food is honey. It's constantly licking the honey off of its paws. **Ursaring** loves to eat berries. The big bear will climb up trees in search of its favorite food. **Ursaring** also has a great sense of smell and can find food buried underground.

Ursaring
Hibernator Pokémon

Pronunciation:
UR-suh-ring

Height: 5' 11"
Weight: 277 lbs

Possible Moves:
Scratch, Leer, Lick, Fury Swipes, Fake Tears, Faint Attack, Rest, Slash, Snore, Thrash

Does not evolve

Teddiursa
Littlebear Pokémon

Pronunciation:
teh-dee-UR-suh

Height: 2' 0"
Weight: 19 lbs

Possible Moves:
Scratch, Leer, Lick, Fury Swipes, Fake Tears, Faint Attack, Rest, Slash, Snore, Thrash

Evolves: at level 30

Igglybuff is the pre-evolved form of the famous singing Pokémon **Jigglypuff**. But **Igglybuff** can't sing yet because its vocal chords aren't developed. **Jigglypuff's** song puts anyone listening to it asleep, which makes **Jigglypuff** very unhappy. It then uses a marker to draw on the faces of its sleeping audience!

Use a Moon Stone to evolve **Jigglypuff** into **Wigglytuff**. It can inflate its rubbery body into an enormous size!

Igglybuff
Balloon Pokémon

Pronunciation:
IG-lee-buff

Possible Moves:
Charm, Sing, Defense Curl, Pound, Sweet Kiss

Evolves: with Friendship

Jigglypuff
Balloon Pokémon

Pronunciation:
JIG-lee-puff

Possible Moves:
Sing, Defense Curl, Pound, Disable, Rollout, Doubleslap, Rest, Body Slam, Mimic, Hyper Voice, Double-Edge

Evolves: with a Moon Stone

Wigglytuff
Balloon Pokémon

Pronunciation:
WIG-lee-tuff

Possible Moves:
Sing, Disable, Defense Curl, Doubleslap

Does not evolve

Igglybuff
Height: 1' 0"
Weight: 2 lbs

Jigglypuff
Height: 1' 8"
Weight: 12 lbs

Wigglytuff
Height: 3' 3"
Weight: 26 lbs

KANTO, JOHTO & HOENN

Meet the charming **Azurill**, the pre-evolved form of the Water Pokémon **Marill** and **Azumarill**. **Azurill** loves to bounce and play on the tip of its rubbery tail. Its tail is packed full of vitamins that help the little Pokémon evolve. **Azurill** can also use its amazing tail to throw itself long distances. In fact, one **Azurill** was able to throw itself a record-breaking 33 feet!

Azurill
Polka Dot Pokémon

Pronunciation:
A-zur-real

Height: 8' 0"
Weight: 4 lbs

Possible Moves:
Splash, Charm, Tail Whip, Bubble, Slam, Water Gun

Evolves: with Friendship

Marill
(Water Type)

Azumarill
(Water Type)

Did somebody say banana? The monkeylike **Aipom** would love one, and it will use its tail to grab it. **Aipom's** tail has a hand on the end. It uses its tail to swing from tree branch to tree branch. **Aipom** relies so much on its tail that it hardly ever uses its real hands. Because of this, **Aipom's** hands are pretty clumsy!

Aipom
Long Tail Pokémon

Pronunciation:
AYE-pom

Possible Moves:
Scratch, Tail Whip, Sand-Attack, Astonish, Baton Pass, Tickle, Fury Swipes, Swift, Screech, Agility

Does not evolve

Aipom
Height: 2' 7"
Weight: 25 lbs

JOHTO

Although **Snubbull** looks tough, this Pokémon is actually very kind and sweet. Women seem to like this Pokémon. They love to pamper and baby the cuddly **Snubbull**. Too scared to battle, **Snubbull** will growl and make scary faces in order to frighten away any enemies. When it evolves into **Granbull**, it becomes even scarier-looking with its huge pair of fangs. But **Granbull** is just as chicken as **Snubbull**!

Snubbull
Fairy Pokémon

Pronunciation:
SNUHB-bull

Height: 2' 0"
Weight: 17 lbs

Possible Moves:
Tackle, Scary Face, Tail Whip, Charm, Bite, Lick, Roar, Rage, Take Down, Crunch

Evolves: at level 23

Granbull
Fairy Pokémon

Pronunciation:
GRAN-bull

Height: 4' 7"
Weight: 107 lbs

Possible Moves:
Tackle, Scary Face, Tail Whip, Charm, Bite, Lick, Roar, Rage, Take Down, Crunch

Does not evolve

Stantler is famous for its amazing antlers. Anyone who stares at them will lose control of their senses and be unable to stand. The curved antlers change the flow of the air around the Pokémon to create a strange space where reality is distorted.

Stantler was once hunted for its beautiful antlers. They were sold at high prices as works of art. Poor **Stantler** was hunted almost to extinction!

Stantler
Big Horn Pokémon

Pronunciation:
STANT-lur

Possible Moves:
Tackle, Leer, Astonish, Hypnosis, Stomp, Sand-Attack, Role Play, Take Down, Confuse Ray, Calm Mind

Does not evolve

Stantler
Height: 4' 7"
Weight: 157 lbs

Smeargle marks the boundaries of its territory, using a paintlike fluid that leaks from the tip of its tail. This painting Pokémon lets other **Smeargle** paint footprints on its back once it's fully grown. **Smeargle's** tail comes in all different colors. If you love to paint, then **Smeargle** is the perfect Pokémon for you! But even if you aren't an artist, **Smeargle** is a great Pokémon to use in battle—the move Sketch lets **Smeargle** learn its opponent's attacks!

Smeargle
Painter Pokémon

Pronunciation:
SMEER-gull

Possible Moves:
Sketch

Does not evolve

Smeargle
Height: 3' 11"
Weight: 128 lbs

Got **Miltank**? Its milk has lots of nutrition and is great for anyone who is sick. But even if you aren't sick, you will love **Miltank**'s sweet, delicious milk.

Miltank produces more than five gallons of milk every day! If you don't like milk, **Miltank**'s milk can be turned into yogurt.

Miltank
Milk Cow Pokémon

Pronunciation:
MILL-tank

Height: 3' 11"
Weight: 166 lbs

Possible Moves:
Tackle, Growl, Defense Curl, Stomp, Milk Drink, Bide, Rollout, Body Slam, Heal Bell

Does not evolve

Tip:
Pink Bow and **Polkadot Bow** are two items that will increase the power of your Normal Pokémon's moves. These two items will also make your Pokémon look cute!

Girafarig is one strange-looking Pokémon. It's hard to tell which is its front and which is its back. Actually, the smaller brown head is the tip of **Girafarig**'s tail! But the tail has a small brain of its own. It attacks in response to smells and sounds. Never approach **Girafarig** from behind. Its sensitive tail will lash out and bite you!

Girafarig
Long Neck Pokémon

Pronunciation:
jir-AFF-uh-rig

Possible Moves:
Tackle, Growl, Astonish, Confusion, Stomp, Odor Sleuth, Agility, Baton Pass, Psybeam, Crunch

Does not evolve

Dual Type:
Normal/Psychic

Girafarig
Height: 4' 11"
Weight: 91 lbs

The curious **Zigzagoon** can't sit still. Wanting to know everything that's going on around it, **Zigzagoon** wanders around, interested in anything it sees. In battle, this Pokémon plays dead, then it attacks!

Linoone, **Zigzagoon**'s evolved form, can run at speeds of 60 miles per hour. But **Linoone** can only run in a straight line! If it needs to turn, it must come to a complete stop first.

Linoone
Rushing Pokémon

Pronunciation:
lih-NOON

Height: 1' 8"
Weight: 72 lbs

Possible Moves:
Tackle, Growl, Tail Whip, Headbutt, Sand-Attack, Odor Sleuth, Mud Sport, Fury Swipes, Covet, Slash, Rest, Belly Drum

Does not evolve

Zigzagoon
Tinyraccoon Pokémon

Pronunciation:
zig-zah-GOON

Height: 1' 4"
Weight: 39 lbs

Possible Moves:
Tackle, Growl, Tail Whip, Headbutt, Sand-Attack, Odor Sleuth, Mud Sport, Pin Missile, Covet, Flail, Rest, Belly Drum

Evolves: at level 20

Slakoth is the ultimate Pokémon couch potato. It loves to loaf around all day. In fact, it moves around so little that it only needs to eat three leaves a day! But that changes when **Slakoth** evolves into **Vigoroth**. The energetic **Vigoroth** can't sit still for a minute. It likes to run through the jungle in a wild rampage. But **Vigoroth** slows down again when it evolves. Lazy **Slaking** lies around all day, eating nearby grass.

Slakoth
Slacker Pokémon

Pronunciation:
slah-KOTH

Possible Moves:
Scratch, Yawn, Encore, Slack Off, Faint Attack, Amnesia, Covet, Counter, Flail

Evolves: at level 18

Vigoroth
Wild Monkey Pokémon

Pronunciation:
vig-AH-roth

Possible Moves:
Scratch, Focus Energy, Encore, Uproar, Fury Swipes, Endure, Slash, Counter, Focus Punch, Reversal

Evolves: at level 36

Slaking
Lazy Pokémon

Pronunciation:
slay-KING

Possible Moves:
Scratch, Yawn, Encore, Slack Off, Faint Attack, Amnesia, Covet, Swagger, Counter, Flail

Does not evolve

Slakoth
Height: 2' 7"
Weight: 53 lbs

Vigoroth
Height: 4' 7"
Weight: 103 lbs

Slaking
Height: 6' 7"
Weight: 288 lbs

HOENN

Shhhh. **Whismur** is trying to talk. This little Pokémon can't talk above a whisper unless it gets upset. Then **Whismur** will cry at an ear-shattering volume. And when it evolves into **Loudred**, grab some earplugs. **Loudred's** best weapon is its loud voice. It can even collapse a house with its shouts! But **Exploud** is the loudest of all. Its shouting can trigger earthquakes!

Whismur
Whisper Pokémon

Pronunciation:
WISS-mur

Possible Moves:
Pound, Uproar, Astonish, Howl, Supersonic, Roar, Stomp, Screech, Rest, Sleep Talk, Hyper Voice

Evolves: at level 20

Loudred
Big Voice Pokémon

Pronunciation:
LOWD-red

Possible Moves:
Pound, Uproar, Astonish, Howl, Supersonic, Roar, Stomp, Screech, Rest, Sleep Talk, Hyper Voice

Evolves: at level 40

Exploud
Loud Noise Pokémon

Pronunciation:
ex-PLOWD

Possible Moves:
Pound, Uproar, Astonish, Howl, Supersonic, Roar, Stomp, Screech, Rest, Hyper Beam, Sleep Talk, Hyper Voice

Does not evolve

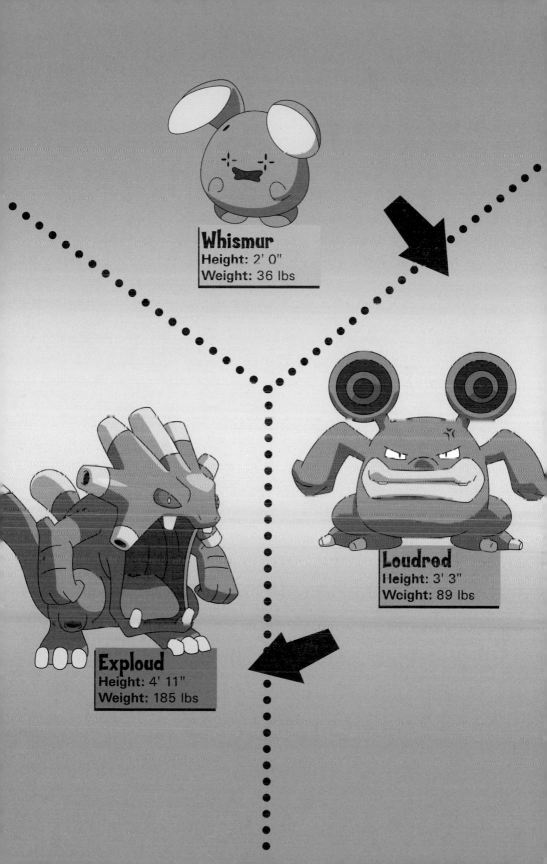

Whismur
Height: 2' 0"
Weight: 36 lbs

Loudred
Height: 3' 3"
Weight: 89 lbs

Exploud
Height: 4' 11"
Weight: 185 lbs

Skitty might be the cutest Pokémon of all. Even Team Rocket's **Meowth** couldn't resist the Kitten Pokémon's charms. **Skitty** loves to chase its tail—and anything else that moves—making it a very popular pet.

More independent than **Skitty**, **Delcatty** likes to do things on its own, whenever it pleases. If you don't want your **Skitty** to evolve, make sure you don't expose it to a Moon Stone!

Skitty
Kitten Pokémon

Pronunciation:
SKIT-tee

Height: 2' 0"
Weight: 24 lbs

Possible Moves:
Growl, Tackle, Tail Whip, Attract, Sing, Doubleslap, Assist, Charm, Faint, Attack, Covet, Heal Bell, Double-Edge

Evolves: with a Moon Stone

Delcatty
Prim Pokémon

Pronunciation:
del-KAT-tee

Height: 3' 7"
Weight: 72 lbs

Possible Moves:
Growl, Attract, Sing, Doubleslap

Does not evolve

Spinda has a very funny walk. Some people say its shaky steps make it look like it's dancing. But others think Spinda stumbles around like it's dizzy. These awkward lurching movements help Spinda in battle by confusing its opponent. And check out the pattern of spots on Spinda. No two Spinda have the same spots—cool!

Spinda
Spot Panda Pokémon

Pronunciation:
SPIN-dah

Height: 3' 7"
Weight: 11 lbs

Possible Moves:
Tackle, Uproar, Faint, Attack, Psybeam, Flail, Hypnosis, Dizzy Punch, Teeter Dance, Psych Up, Double-Edge, Thrash

Does not evolve

Tip:
A **Moon Stone** is a useful item to have for several Normal Pokémon. You can use it to evolve **Clefairy, Jigglypuff,** and **Skitty.**

Zangoose is fast on its feet. It can dodge almost any attack. Zangoose walks around on all fours unless it's furious. Then it stands on its hind legs and extends its sharp claws. What makes Zangoose angry? Seviper, Zangoose's worst enemy, does. Whenever these two Pokémon meet, they have a fierce battle!

Zangoose
Cat Ferret Pokémon

Pronunciation:
ZAN-goose

Possible Moves:
Scratch, Leer, Quick Attack, Swords Dance, Fury Cutter, Slash, Pursuit, Crush Claw, Taunt, Detect, False Swipe

Does not evolve

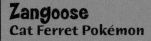

Zangoose
Height: 4' 3"
Weight: 89 lbs

If you see a rain cloud in the sky, look again. It just might be a **Castform**. This weather Pokémon can disguise itself as rain clouds and snow clouds and even the sun. How does **Castform** do this? It's able to borrow the power of nature to protect its tiny body. Not only does **Castform**'s appearance change with the weather, but its mood does, too. If you have a bright, sunny day, you have a happy **Castform**.

Castform
Weather Pokémon

Pronunciation:
CAST-form

Possible Moves:
Tackle, Water Gun, Ember, Powder Snow, Rain Dance, Sunny Day, Hail, Weather Ball

Does not evolve

Castform
Height: 1' 0"
Weight: 2 lbs

Your mom is looking for you. She wants you to clean your room. You lean against the wall, and suddenly your body changes color to match it. You are now totally hidden! That's exactly how **Kecleon** protects itself. It hides from its enemies. **Kecleon** also blends in with its surroundings to sneak up on its target and attack! Then it uses its long, stretchy tongue to catch its prey.

Kecleon
Color Swap Pokémon

Pronunciation:
KEHK-lee-on

Possible Moves:
Thief, Tail Whip, Astonish, Lick, Scratch, Bind, Faint Attack, Fury Swipes, Psybeam, Screech, Slash, Substitute, Ancientpower

Does not evolve

Kecleon
Height: 3' 3"
Weight: 49 lbs

More Dual Type
Normal/Flying Pokémon

There are lots of Normal Pokémon—so many that we couldn't fit them all in this book! So we put these Normal/Flying Pokémon in a handy chart for you.

Many of these Normal/Flying Types look like birds you might see in the park. But don't be fooled. They are all great in battle.

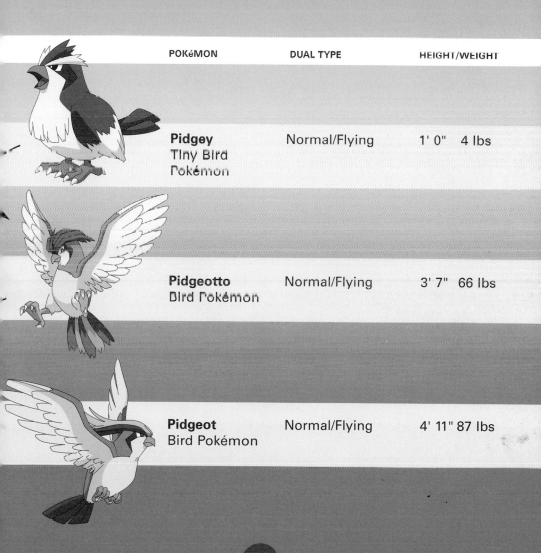

POKÉMON	DUAL TYPE	HEIGHT/WEIGHT
Pidgey Tiny Bird Pokémon	Normal/Flying	1' 0" 4 lbs
Pidgeotto Bird Pokémon	Normal/Flying	3' 7" 66 lbs
Pidgeot Bird Pokémon	Normal/Flying	4' 11" 87 lbs

Spearow
Tiny Bird Pokémon — Normal/Flying — 1' 0" 4 lbs

Fearow
Beak Pokémon — Normal/Flying — 3' 11" 84 lbs

Farfetch'd
Wild Duck
Pokémon — Normal/Flying — 2' 7" 33 lbs

Hoothoot
Owl Pokémon — Normal/Flying — 2' 4" 47 lbs

Noctowl
Owl Pokémon — Normal/Flying — 5' 3" 90 lbs

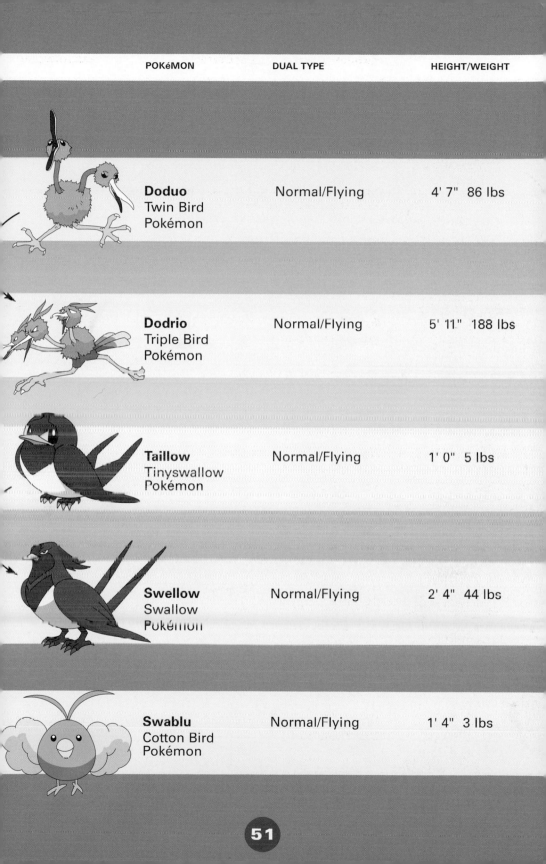

Doduo
Twin Bird
Pokémon

Normal/Flying

4' 7" 86 lbs

Dodrio
Triple Bird
Pokémon

Normal/Flying

5' 11" 188 lbs

Taillow
Tinyswallow
Pokémon

Normal/Flying

1' 0" 5 lbs

Swellow
Swallow
Pokémon

Normal/Flying

2' 4" 44 lbs

Swablu
Cotton Bird
Pokémon

Normal/Flying

1' 4" 3 lbs

A Gym for Normal Pokémon

Are you eager to see some Normal Pokémon in action? Or maybe you want to battle a Normal Pokémon yourself? Then head to Petalburg City in the Hoenn region. The Petalburg City Gym is a haven for Normal Pokémon!

But before you get to battle the Gym Leader, you will have to battle a few Trainers first. You will face a **Delcatty**, **Linoone**, and **Zangoose**.

Then it's on to battle Norman, the Gym Leader. He is the father of Ash's friends, Max and May. Norman has a **Vigoroth** and a **Slaking** that are hard to beat. But if you have some Fighting Types on your team, you might just win. Then Norman will give you a Balance Badge.

Ash battled Norman for a Balance Badge. In the end, Ash's **Grovyle** took out **Slaking** after a tough fight. Poor Max! He was really upset that his dad lost the battle. But Norman explained that even Gym Leaders lose, that Ash is a good Trainer, and that he won fair and square.

Then Max felt better. He joined Ash, May, and Brock on their Pokémon journey. Now the friends are always together. They are ready for any challenge that comes their way—even hard-to-beat Normal Pokémon!

Meet Meowth

Meowth is a member of Team Rocket. This team of thieves travels around, trying to steal Pokémon. They also try to make money with their crazy schemes. We talked to **Meowth** about his life with Team Rocket. Here's what he had to say:

You are one of the few Pokémon who can talk. How did you learn to speak?

I did it for love! I was in love with a **Meowth** named Meowzie. I wanted to impress her, so I learned how to talk. But she just thought I was a freak, and my poor little heart was broken!

Why did you join Team Rocket?

When Meowzie broke my heart, I was all alone in da world. Jessie and James took me in. I don't want to sound mushy or nothin', but they're my best friends!

Is it true that you are the real brains behind Team Rocket?

You betta believe it! Jessie and James couldn't tie their shoes without me. I come up with all the best plans.

So is it your fault when all of the plans go wrong?

No way! It's that twerp Ash and his friends who ruin everything.

You might act tough, but we hear you have a sweet side, Meowth.

Well, I mighta saved a certain **Skitty** from a life of crime with Team Rocket. And maybe I've done a few other things I'm ashamed to admit. Just don't spread it around, okay?

Your secret's safe with us, Meowth. Thanks for talking to us!

No problem!

Back to Normal!

Now that you have read this section, you could go back to your normal life of school, homework, and cleaning your room. Or, you could explore the world of Normal Pokémon. You could search the starry skies to find a **Cleffa**. You could scan the treetops for an **Aipom**. Or you could surf cyberspace for a **Porygon** of your very own.

Whatever you choose to do, you are bound to have strange and unusual adventures. Because now you know that training Normal Pokémon can be fun and exciting!

Once you catch a Normal Type, check out www.Pokémon.com for more cool information about caring for it. The world of Normal Pokémon is waiting for you!

Get Psyched!

Take the mystery out of the mysterious and strange world of Psychic Type Pokémon. Here is what you will find in this *Pokédex*:

* Stats for 44 Psychic Pokémon.
* The story of the battle between **Mew** and **Mewtwo**.
* The scoop on the best Psychic Gym Leaders.
* A talk with James from Team Rocket.

So don't be psyched out by Psychic Pokémon. Instead, open your mind and discover their power. Learn to respect them, and after you finish this section, you might just become a Psychic Pokémon Master!

You Are Getting Sleepy....

So wake up! It's time to learn about some of the most unusual and powerful Pokémon around—Psychic Types.

What makes these Pokémon so unusual and powerful? Maybe it's their amazing powers. Psychic Types can hypnotize you, make you see things that aren't real, and control your mind. They can travel through time and grant wishes. And then there's **Unown**. This Pokémon might even make a person's dreams come true!

Psychic Types are some of the hardest Pokémon to catch and beat in battle. Just try to capture **Mew** or **Mewtwo** and see what we mean.

While it's easy to find Pokémon like **Pidgey** in the wild, Psychic Pokémon are usually hard to track down. That might be because scientists don't know where many of them came from. They think that **Celebi** traveled to our time from the future. And it's likely that **Deoxys** came from outer space!

If you are a Pokémon Trainer, you don't need a crystal ball to tell you that it's a good idea to have some of these amazing Pokémon on your team. Good luck finding them! You will definitely have to be smart to catch one.

Even if you don't want to train a Psychic Type, it's still a good idea to know what makes them tick. You will probably meet some Psychic Type Trainers on your journey. Some are a little bit weird! But if you read this book, you will learn how to defeat them.

So get ready to enter the strange world of Psychic Pokémon. And don't worry about getting sleepy. The stuff you are about to read is so exciting that it will probably keep you awake at night!

Battle Tips for Psychic Types

One of the things a Pokémon Trainer needs to know is which Pokémon to choose in a battle. If you battle with a Psychic Pokémon, this chart will help you to know which moves will do the most—or the least—damage to other Pokémon.

Psychic Types Are Good Against:
* Fighting Types such as **Machop**.
* Poison Types such as **Swalot**.

Psychic Types
Are Bad Against:

✳ Steel Types such as **Registeel**.

✳ Other Psychic Types such as **Mr. Mime**.

✳ Dark Types such as **Absol**. Psychic moves
do no damage to Dark Pokémon!

You can enjoy **Mr. Mime**'s pantomime act all you want—just don't interrupt it! If you disturb **Mr. Mime** while it's doing its routine, it will slap you with its big hands!

When **Mr. Mime** moves its hands, it can make you think an object is there that really isn't. Once the enemy believes it's true, the item becomes real! This is very useful in battle.

Mr. Mime
Barrier Pokémon

Pronunciation:
MISS-tur MEYEM

Possible Moves:
Barrier, Confusion, Substitute, Meditate, Doubleslap, Light Screen, Reflect, Magical Leaf, Encore, Psybeam, Recycle, Trick, Role Play, Psychic, Baton Pass, Safeguard

Does not evolve

Mr. Mime
Height: 4' 3"
Weight: 120 lbs

You can't claim to be a Pokémon Master until you have captured the Legendary **Mewtwo**. Scientists used the cells of the rare **Mew** to try to create a Pokémon that couldn't be destroyed. But **Mewtwo** is so strong that the scientists had created a Pokémon so powerful and intelligent that even *they* couldn't control it.

If you think you have what it takes to catch **Mewtwo**, you had better come with your Master Ball and your strongest Pokémon!

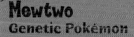

Mewtwo
Genetic Pokémon

Pronunciation:
MYOO-too

Possible Moves:
Confusion, Disable, Barrier, Mist, Swift, Recover, Amnesia, Safeguard, Psychic, Psych Up, Future Sight

Does not evolve

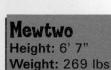

Mewtwo
Height: 6' 7"
Weight: 269 lbs

Believed to be the ancestor of all Pokémon, **Mew** is the most Legendary Pokémon ever. For years, people thought **Mew** was just a fairy tale. But then people began spotting the pink Pokémon.

Have you been lucky enough to catch a glimpse of **Mew**? If so, it means you have a pure heart. And if you can actually catch **Mew**, your opponents had better watch out—**Mew** can learn Metronome, which means almost anything can happen in battle!

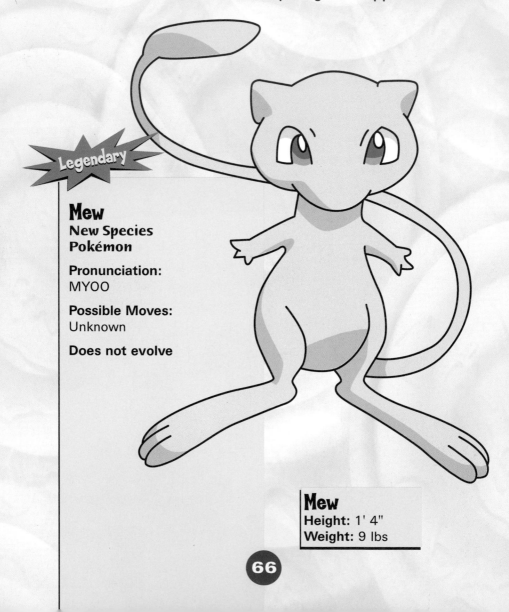

Legendary

Mew
New Species Pokémon

Pronunciation:
MYOO

Possible Moves:
Unknown

Does not evolve

Mew
Height: 1' 4"
Weight: 9 lbs

Have you ever woken up and been craving a midnight snack? You probably wanted milk and cookies. But not **Drowzee**—it munches on dreams! **Drowzee** perfects the art of dream-eating when it evolves into **Hypno**. Using a shiny object, **Hypno** can put you to sleep by swinging it back and forth. Then it gobbles up your dreams!

Drowzee
Hypnosis Pokémon

Pronunciation:
DROW-zee

Height: 3' 3"
Weight: 71 lbs

Possible Moves:
Pound, Hypnosis, Disable, Confusion, Headbutt, Poison Gas, Meditate, Psychic, Psych Up, Swagger, Future Sight

Evolves: at level 26

Hypno
Hypnosis Pokémon

Pronunciation:
HIP-noh

Height: 5' 3"
Weight: 167 lbs

Possible Moves:
Nightmare, Pound, Psych Up, Hypnosis, Disable, Confusion, Headbutt, Poison Gas, Meditate, Psychic, Swagger, Future Sight

Does not evolve

If you are looking for a Pokémon to do your homework, then **Slowpoke** is *not* for you! When something bites its tail, it takes about 5 seconds for dopey **Slowpoke** to feel it. **Shellder** loves to bite **Slowpoke**'s tail. Once attached, **Shellder** won't let go, which is how **Slowpoke** evolves into **Slowbro**. But **Slowbro** isn't any smarter than **Slowpoke**. If you really want a supersmart Pokémon, you will need **Slowking**—one of the smartest Pokémon around.

Slowpoke
Dopey Pokémon

Pronunciation:
SLOH-pohk

Possible Moves:
Curse, Tackle, Yawn, Psychic, Growl, Water Gun, Psych Up, Confusion, Disable, Headbutt, Amnesia

Evolves: at level 37 into **Slowbro** or with a Trade while holding a King's Rock into **Slowking**

Slowbro
Hermit Crab Pokémon

Pronunciation:
SLOH-broh

Possible Moves:
Curse, Tackle, Yawn, Growl, Water Gun, Psych Up, Confusion, Disable, Headbutt, Amnesia, Withdraw, Psychic

Does not evolve

Slowking
Royal Pokémon

Pronunciation:
SLOH-king

Possible Moves:
Curse, Tackle, Yawn, Growl, Water Gun, Psych Up, Confusion, Disable, Headbutt, Swagger, Psychic

Does not evolve

Dual Type: Water/Psychic

Slowpoke
Height: 3' 11"
Weight: 79 lbs

Dual Type:
Water/Psychic

Dual Type:
Water/Psychic

Slowking
Height: 6' 7"
Weight: 175 lbs

Slowbro
Height: 5' 3"
Weight: 173 lbs

Exeggcute are egglike Pokémon that come together in groups of six. These are tough little Pokémon—their shells are really hard to crack. And if you threaten them, they will attack in a swarm.

When **Exeggcute** evolves into **Exeggutor**, it looks like a walking palm tree with egg-shaped heads. When its heads fall off, they become another **Exeggcute**.

Exeggutor
Coconut Pokémon

Pronunciation:
EGGS-egg-you-tore

Height: 6' 7"
Weight: 265 lbs

Possible Moves:
Barrage, Hypnosis, Stomp, Confusion, Egg Bomb

Does not evolve

Dual Type: Grass/Psychic

Exeggcute
Egg Pokémon

Pronunciation:
EGGS-egg-kuoot

Height: 1' 4"
Weight: 6 lbs

Possible Moves:
Barrage, Hypnosis, Stun Spore, Reflect, Leech Seed, Poisonpowder, Sleep Powder, Uproar, Solarbeam, Confusion

Evolves: with a Leaf Stone

Dual Type: Grass/Psychic

Pucker up—here comes a **Smoochum**! Its supersensitive lips help **Smoochum** to identify things. And **Smoochum** always rocks its head back and forth as if it's trying to give someone a kiss.

Jynx is the evolved form of **Smoochum**. **Jynx** sways its hips back and forth as it walks. If a **Jynx** walks by, you feel like dancing!

Dual Type: Ice/Psychic

Jynx
Human Shape Pokémon

Pronunciation: JINKS

Height: 4' 7"
Weight: 90 lbs

Possible Moves: Pound, Lick, Lovely Kiss, Powder Snow, Ice Punch, Doubleslap, Mean Look, Fake Tears, Body Slam, Perish Song, Blizzard

Does not evolve

Dual Type: Ice/Psychic

Smoochum
Kiss Pokémon

Pronunciation: SMOOCH-uhm

Height: 1'4"
Weight: 14 lbs

Possible Moves: Pound, Lick, Sweet Kiss, Powder Snow, Blizzard, Confusion, Sing, Mean Look, Fake Tears, Perish Song, Psychic

Evolves: at level 30

Imagine a Pokémon that can predict its opponent's next move—or even the weather. That's **Espeon**. The tip of **Espeon**'s forked tail quivers when it's sensing what is about to happen next. This evolved form of **Eevee** is very loyal to a Trainer who treats it right. In fact, **Espeon** will use its psychic abilities to protect its Trainer from any harm. So if you want to know if you will need an umbrella for the day or if you just want to win a battle, **Espeon** has what it takes!

Eevee
(Normal Type)

Espeon
Sun Pokémon

Pronunciation:
EHS-pee-on

Height: 2' 11"
Weight: 58 lbs

Possible Moves:
Tackle, Tail Whip, Helping Hand, Sand-Attack, Confusion, Quick Attack, Swift, Psybeam, Psych Up, Psychic, Morning Sun

Does not evolve

KANTO & JOHTO

You may know your ABC's—but do you know the **Unown** alphabet? This Psychic Pokémon can be one of 28 different shapes—a different shape for each letter of our alphabet, plus a question mark and an exclamation point! One of the most mysterious Pokémon, **Unown** looks like hieroglyphics, an ancient form of writing. **Unown's** flat, thin body likes to stick to walls. If you didn't know what **Unown** looked like, you would walk right past it, thinking somebody had written on the wall!

Unown
Symbol Pokémon

Pronunciation:
UHN-nohn

Height: 1' 8"
Weight: 11 lbs

Possible Moves:
Hidden Power

Does not evolve

Abra likes to sleep for 18 hours a day. It can sleep at any time and in any place and remain completely safe. What's Abra's secret? If Abra senses danger, it teleports itself away, even while it's sleeping.

When Abra evolves into Kadabra, it learns other ways to protect itself. For instance, just being close to Kadabra can cause terrible headaches. When Kadabra evolves into Alakazam, it becomes super-smart—with an I.Q. of 5,000!

Abra
Psi Pokémon

Pronunciation:
AB-ruh

Possible Moves:
Teleport

Evolves: at level 16

Kadabra
Psi Pokémon

Pronunciation:
kuh-DAH-bruh

Possible Moves:
Teleport, Kinesis, Trick, Confusion, Disable, Psybeam, Reflect, Recover, Future Sight, Role Play, Psychic

Evolves: with a Trade

Alakazam
Psi Pokémon

Pronunciation:
al-uh-kuh-ZAM

Possible Moves:
Teleport, Kinesis, Confusion, Disable, Psybeam, Reflect, Recover, Future Sight, Calm Mind, Psychic, Trick

Does not evolve

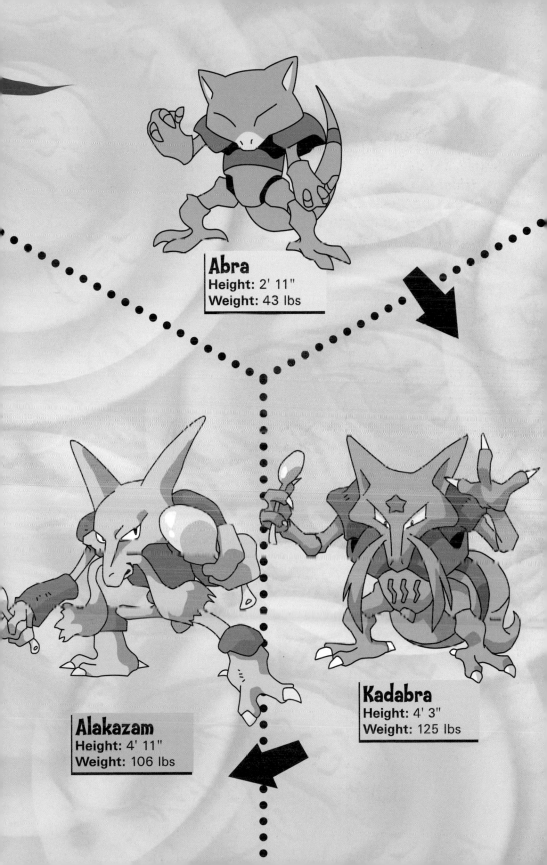

Abra
Height: 2' 11"
Weight: 43 lbs

Kadabra
Height: 4' 3"
Weight: 125 lbs

Alakazam
Height: 4' 11"
Weight: 106 lbs

If you wish upon this star to win your battle, your wish might be granted—if you have a **Starmie** on your team! **Starmie** combines Water attacks with Psychic to pack a powerful punch. The core at the center of **Starmie's** body glows in seven different colors.

Is it using these colors to talk to other **Starmie**, or is it sending messages to outer space? We might never know.

Staryu
(Water Type)

Starmie
Mysterious Pokémon

Dual Type:
Water/Psychic

Pronunciation:
STAR-mee

Possible Moves:
Water Gun, Rapid Spin, Recover, Swift, Confuse Ray

Does not evolve

Starmie
Height: 3' 7"
Weight: 176 lbs

Tiny **Natu** hops around on the ground. Its wings aren't fully grown, so it can't fly. If you look into **Natu's** eyes, it will stare back at you and not blink. But if you move toward **Natu**, it will hop away to safety.

Natu evolves into the mystical **Xatu**. This Psychic Pokémon can see into both the past and future. **Xatu** will stand in one spot all day long meditating.

Xatu
Mystic Pokémon

Pronunciation:
ZAH-too

Height: 4' 11"
Weight: 33 lbs

Dual Type:
Psychic/Flying

Possible Moves:
Peck, Leer, Night Shade, Teleport, Wish, Future Sight, Confuse Ray, Psychic

Does not evolve

Natu
Tiny Bird Pokémon

Pronunciation:
NAH-too

Dual Type:
Psychic/Flying

Height: 0' 8"
Weight: 4 lbs

Possible Moves:
Peck, Leer, Night Shade, Teleport, Wish, Future Sight, Confuse Ray, Psychic

Evolves: at level 25

Wynaut always has a happy smile on its face, even if it's in a bad mood. So how can you tell if this Psychic Pokémon is angry? Look at its tail. If **Wynaut** is slapping the ground with its tail, it's definitely mad!

Wobbuffet, the evolved form of **Wynaut**, likes to keep its dark black tail hidden. This is why **Wobbuffet** prefers to live in dark places, like caves. It is a very competitive Pokémon. When two **Wobbuffet** meet, they will compete to see who has more endurance.

Wobbuffet
Patient Pokémon

Pronunciation:
WAH-buh-feht

Possible Moves:
Counter, Mirror Coat, Safeguard, Destiny Bond

Does not evolve

Wynaut
Bright Pokémon

Pronunciation:
WY-not

Possible Moves:
Splash, Charm, Encore, Counter, Mirror Coat, Safeguard, Destiny Bond

Evolves: at level 15

Wynaut
Height: 2' 0"
Weight: 31 lbs

Wobbuffet
Height: 4' 3"
Weight: 63 lbs

Tip:
Jessie from Team Rocket has a **Wobbuffet**. This Psychic Pokémon is extremely loyal but always pops out at the wrong time!

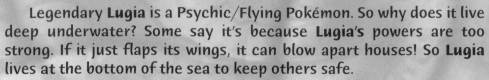

JOHTO

Legendary **Lugia** is a Psychic/Flying Pokémon. So why does it live deep underwater? Some say it's because **Lugia's** powers are too strong. If it just flaps its wings, it can blow apart houses! So **Lugia** lives at the bottom of the sea to keep others safe.

Lugia is known as the guardian of the seas. If a bad storm starts, **Lugia** is able to calm it. That's why the best time to see this rare Pokémon is the night of a storm.

Lugia
Diving Pokémon

Dual Type: Psychic/Flying

Legendary

Pronunciation:
loo-GEE-uh

Possible Moves:
Unknown

Does not evolve

Lugia
Height: 17' 1"
Weight: 476 lbs

Lugia is known as guardian of the sea, and **Celebi** is known as guardian of the forest. That's because wherever **Celebi** travels, it helps trees to grow. **Celebi** has another amazing ability. It can travel through time!

Some believe that **Celebi** came to our time from the future. If you see this Pokémon, it means your future is bright!

Legendary

Celebi
Time Travel Pokémon

Dual Type:
Grass/Psychic

Pronunciation:
SELL-uh-bee

Possible Moves:
Unknown

Does not evolve

Celebi
Height: 2' 0"
Weight: 11 lbs

Girafarig has one of the most unusual tails in the Pokémon world. The tip of its tail is actually an extra head! **Girafarig's** extra head has a very small brain and mostly responds to smells and sounds. So if you walk near a **Girafarig's** tail and it smells you, watch out! It might bite you with its sharp little teeth.

Girafarig
Long Neck Pokémon

Pronunciation:
jir-AFF-uh-rig

Dual Type:
Normal/Psychic

Possible Moves:
Tackle, Growl, Astonish, Confusion, Stomp, Odor Sleuth, Agility, Baton Pass, Psybeam, Crunch

Does not evolve

Girafarig
Height: 4' 11"
Weight: 91 lbs

Meditite and Medicham have a special way to train. They go to the mountains and meditate. This increases their inner energy. When Meditite evolves, Medicham develops a sixth sense. This gives Medicham special psychic powers. It can even hide by blending with hills and mountains.

Meditite
Meditate Pokémon

Dual Type: Fighting/Psychic

Pronunciation: MED-uh-teyet

Height: 2' 0"
Weight: 25 lbs

Possible Moves:
Bide, Meditate, Confusion, Detect, Hidden Power, Swagger, Mind Reader, Calm Mind, Hi Jump Kick, Psych Up, Reversal, Recover

Evolves: at level 37

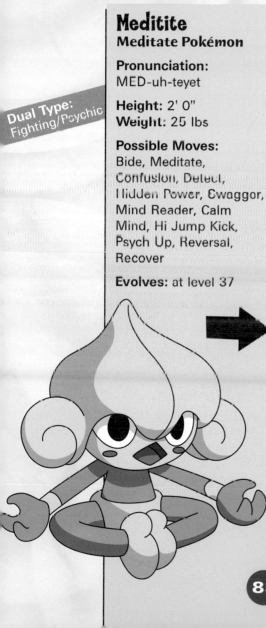

Medicham
Meditate Pokémon

Dual Type: Fighting/Psychic

Pronunciation: MED-uh-cham

Height: 4' 3"
Weight: 69 lbs

Possible Moves:
Fire Punch, Thunderpunch, Ice Punch, Bide, Meditate, Confusion, Detect, Swagger, Hidden Power, Mind Reader, Calm Mind, Hi Jump Kick, Psych Up, Reversal, Recover

Does not evolve

Ralts uses the horns on its head to sense how people feel. If its Trainer is happy, Ralts is happy, too. Kirlia, Ralt's evolved form, also uses its horns to increase its psychic power. When Kirlia's Trainer is happy, this Pokémon grows more beautiful.

Gardevoir is very loyal to its Trainer. If Gardevoir's Trainer is in danger, Gardevoir lets loose with all of its psychic power!

Kirlia
Emotion Pokémon

Pronunciation:
kur-LEE-ah

Possible Moves:
Magical Leaf, Growl, Confusion, Double Team, Teleport, Calm Mind, Psychic, Imprison, Future Sight, Hypnosis, Dream Eater

Evolves: at level 30

Ralts
Feeling Pokémon

Pronunciation:
RAWLTZ

Possible Moves:
Growl, Confusion, Double Team, Teleport, Calm Mind, Psychic, Imprison, Future Sight, Hypnosis, Dream Eater

Evolves: at level 20

Gardevoir
Embrace Pokémon

Pronunciation:
GAR-deh-vor

Possible Moves:
Growl, Confusion, Double Team, Teleport, Calm Mind, Psychic, Imprison, Future Sight, Hypnosis, Dream Eater

Does not evolve

Ralts
Height: 1' 4"
Weight: 15 lbs

Gardevoir
Height: 5' 3"
Weight: 107 lbs

Kirlia
Height: 2' 7"
Weight: 45 lbs

What's that on top of **Spoink**'s head? It's a pearl—a very special pearl. It makes **Spoink**'s psychic powers stronger. That's why **Spoink** is always looking for a bigger pearl. It wants more power!

Grumpig, **Spoink**'s evolved form, has black pearls all over its body. These pearls also make **Grumpig**'s powers stronger. With its pearls, this Pokémon can gain total control over an enemy. **Grumpig**'s pearls are also prized as works of art!

Spoink
Bounce Pokémon

Pronunciation:
SPOINK

Possible Moves:
Splash, Psywave, Odor Sleuth, Psybeam, Psych Up, Confuse Ray, Magic Coat, Psychic, Rest, Snore, Bounce

Evolves: at level 32

Grumpig
Manipulate Pokémon

Pronunciation:
gruhm-PIG

Possible Moves:
Splash, Psywave, Odor Sleuth, Psybeam, Psych Up, Confuse Ray, Magic Coat, Psychic, Rest, Snore, Bounce

Does not evolve

Spoink
Height: 2' 4"
Weight: 67 lbs

Tip:
Would you let your Psychic Pokémon take a nap in the middle of a battle? It sounds crazy. But if you teach it the move **Rest**, you can let your Pokémon sleep through two turns of a battle. This way, it will regain health points.

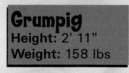

Grumpig
Height: 2' 11"
Weight: 158 lbs

Is **Lunatone** from outer space? No one's sure. The Rock/Psychic Pokémon was found in a place where a meteorite fell.

When the moon is full, **Lunatone** begins to move, floating in midair. If you are out when there's a full moon and you look at **Lunatone's** glowing red eyes, you will become frozen with fear. So watch out!

Lunatone
Meteorite Pokémon

Pronunciation:
LOO-na-tohn

Possible Moves:
Tackle, Harden, Confusion, Rock Throw, Hypnosis, Psywave, Cosmic Power, Psychic, Future Sight, Explosion

Does not evolve

Dual Type:
Rock/Psychic

Lunatone
Height: 3' 3"
Weight: 370 lbs

Like **Lunatone**, **Solrock** floats in the air. It doesn't make a sound. But while **Lunatone** gets power from the moon, **Solrock** gets its power from the sun. This Rock/Psychic Pokémon's body gives off a lot of heat. In battle, it releases a really bright light. And that isn't all **Solrock** can do. It can tell how people and Pokémon are feeling when they are nearby.

Solrock
Meteorite Pokémon

Dual Type: Rock/Psychic

Pronunciation:
SOHL-rock

Possible Moves:
Tackle, Harden, Confusion, Rock Throw, Fire Spin, Psywave, Cosmic Power, Rock Slide, Solarbeam, Explosion

Does not evolve

Solrock
Height: 3' 11"
Weight: 340 lbs

Scientists found ancient cave paintings showing **Baltoy** living with humans. The history of **Claydol**, **Baltoy**'s evolved form, is even more unusual. Scientists believe that people made **Claydol** out of mud 20,000 years ago. Then a mysterious ray brought it to life! **Claydol** can float above the ground, shooting beams from its hands.

Baltoy
Clay Doll Pokémon

Pronunciation:
BALL-toy

Height: 1' 8"
Weight: 47 lbs

Possible Moves:
Confusion, Harden, Rapid Spin, Mud-Slap, Psybeam, Rock Tomb, Selfdestruct, Ancientpower, Sandstorm, Cosmic Power, Explosion

Evolves: at level 36

Dual Type:
Ground/Psychic

Claydol
Clay Doll Pokémon

Pronunciation:
KLAY-doll

Height: 4' 11"
Weight: 238 lbs

Possible Moves:
Teleport, Confusion, Mud-Slap, Harden, Rapid Spin, Psybeam, Rock Tomb, Selfdestruct, Sandstorm, Ancientpower, Hyper Beam, Cosmic Power, Explosion

Does not evolve

Dual Type:
Ground/Psychic

What's that eerie sound? It might be a **Chimecho**. This Pokémon likes to hang from trees by a suction cup on its head. If the wind blows, **Chimecho** cries out. In battle, **Chimecho**'s cries can be dangerous. When this Pokémon is angry, its cries are so strong that they can send its opponent flying!

Chimecho
Wind Chime Pokémon

Pronunciation:
chim-EH-koh

Possible Moves:
Wrap, Growl, Astonish, Confusion, Take Down, Uproar, Yawn, Psywave, Double-Edge, Heal Bell, Safeguard, Psychic

Does not evolve

Chimecho
Height: 2' 0"
Weight: 2 lbs

These Pokémon are an unusual blend of Steel and Psychic Types. A powerful magnetic force flows through **Beldum's** body. It uses this force to communicate with others. When two **Beldum** join together, they become a **Metang**. Its two brains have a very strong psychic power. When two **Metangs** fuse together, they evolve into **Metagross**. This Pokémon's four brains are superpowerful—more powerful than some computers!

Metagross
Iron Leg Pokémon

Pronunciation:
MEH-tuh-gross

Possible Moves:
Take Down, Confusion, Metal Claw, Pursuit, Scary Face, Psychic, Iron Defense, Meteor Mash, Agility, Hyper Beam

Does not evolve

Beldum
Iron Ball Pokémon

Pronunciation:
BELL-dum

Possible Moves:
Take Down

Evolves: at level 20

Metang
Iron Claw Pokémon

Pronunciation:
meh-TANG

Possible Moves:
Take Down, Confusion, Metal Claw, Scary Face, Pursuit, Psychic, Iron Defense, Meteor Mash, Agility, Hyper Beam

Evolves: at level 45

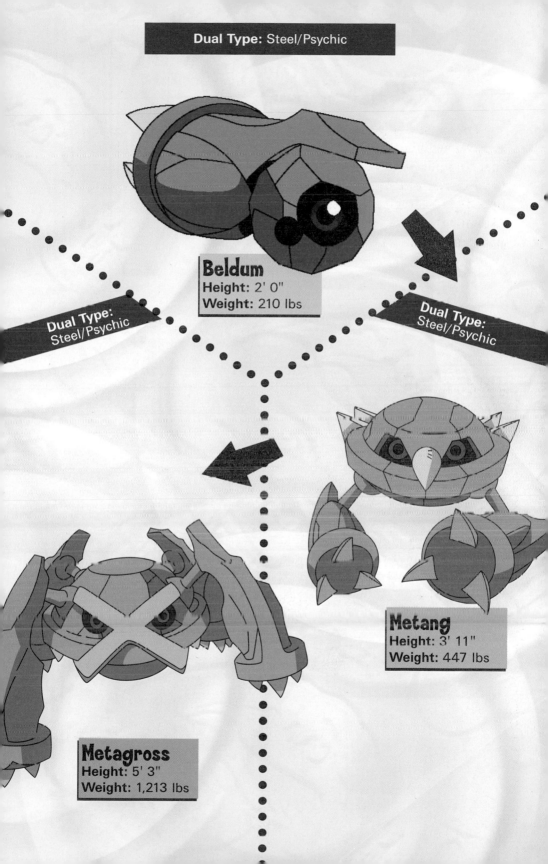

Dual Type: Steel/Psychic

Beldum
Height: 2' 0"
Weight: 210 lbs

Dual Type:
Steel/Psychic

Dual Type:
Steel/Psychic

Metang
Height: 3' 11"
Weight: 447 lbs

Metagross
Height: 5' 3"
Weight: 1,213 lbs

Latias is one of the Legendary Bird Pokémon. It's very smart. In fact, **Latias** is so smart that it can telepathically communicate with humans.

Latias's feathers are made of a material like glass. So when **Latias** doesn't want to be seen, it uses its feathers to distort the light that hits them. This changes the way **Latias** looks.

Latias
Eon Pokémon

Pronunciation:
LAH-tee-us

Legendary

Possible Moves:
Psywave, Wish, Helping Hand, Safeguard, Dragonbreath, Water Sport, Refresh, Mist Ball, Psychic, Recover, Charm

Does not evolve

Dual Type:
Dragon/Psychic

Latias
Height: 4' 7"
Weight: 88 lbs

94

Like **Latias**, **Latios** is very smart. If **Latios** imagines something in its head, it can make its enemy see the same thing. **Latios** can also fly superfast—faster than a jet plane! No wonder **Latios** is a Legendary Pokémon.

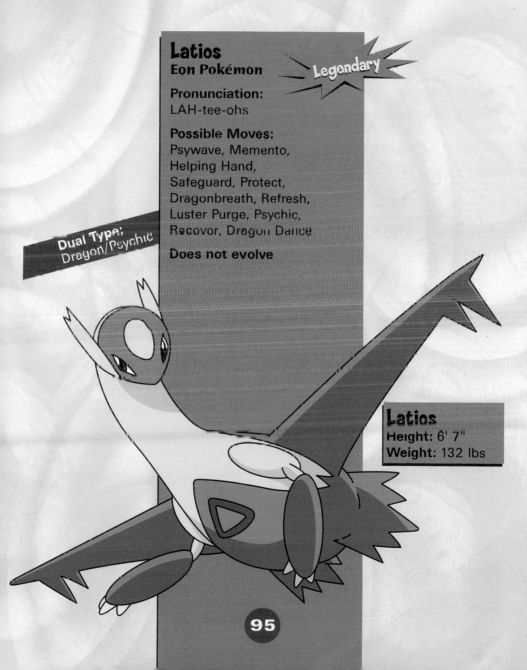

Latios
Eon Pokémon

Legendary

Pronunciation:
LAH-tee-ohs

Possible Moves:
Psywave, Memento, Helping Hand, Safeguard, Protect, Dragonbreath, Refresh, Luster Purge, Psychic, Recover, Dragon Dance

Does not evolve

Dual Type:
Dragon/Psychic

Latios
Height: 6' 7"
Weight: 132 lbs

Jirachi is a rare and special Pokémon that sleeps for 1,000 years. It wakes up only if someone sings it a special song in a pure voice. When Jirachi is awake, legend says it will grant wishes. Then it goes back to sleep again for 1,000 years. If Jirachi is attacked while it's sleeping, it fights back—without even waking up!

Jirachi
Wish Pokémon

Legendary

Dual Type: Steel/Psychic

Pronunciation:
jur-AH-chee

Possible Moves:
Wish, Confusion, Rest, Double-Edge, Swift, Future Sight, Helping Hand, Cosmic Power, Psychic, Doom Desire, Refresh

Does not evolve

Jirachi
Height: 1' 0"
Weight: 2 lbs

You know what a virus is, right? It's a tiny organism that can make you sick—like with a cold. Well, **Deoxys** started out as a virus that was floating around in space. Then it got hit by a laser beam—*bam!*— **Deoxys** was born. This Pokémon won't make you sneeze, but it can shoot lasers from the crystal on its chest.

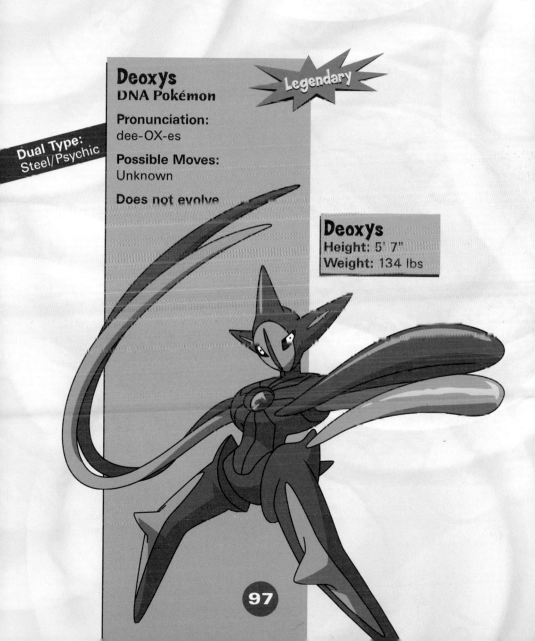

Deoxys
DNA Pokémon

Legendary

Dual Type:
Steel/Psychic

Pronunciation:
dee-OX-es

Possible Moves:
Unknown

Does not evolve

Deoxys
Height: 5' 7"
Weight: 134 lbs

Battle Hall of Fame:
Mew vs. Mewtwo

Which do you think is stronger—**Mew** or **Mewtwo**? Pokémon fans still argue about this. **Mew** came first. Then scientists cloned **Mewtwo** from **Mew's** DNA. They changed the DNA to make **Mewtwo** superpowerful. But is it really stronger than **Mew**? These two Pokémon battled when **Mewtwo** escaped from the lab where it was created. **Mewtwo** then cloned an army of Pokémon to take over the world.

Ash and his friends used their Pokémon to battle **Mewtwo's** army. Ash wanted to stop the battle and ran onto the field to fight **Mewtwo**. The genetic Pokémon sent Ash flying into the air. But Ash was saved . . .

. . . by **Mew**! The small pink Pokémon had sensed the battle and came to help. **Mew** tried to tell **Mewtwo** to stop fighting.

Mewtwo wouldn't listen and hurled blasts of Psychic energy at **Mew**. Fortunately, **Mew** dodged them. Until ...

Bam! One ball of Psychic energy hit **Mew**. The little Pokémon hurtled through space ... **Mew** then hurled the Psychic energy ball back at **Mewtwo**, which protected itself with a bubble of blue energy. The battle was on!

Mew protected itself with a pink bubble. The two Pokémon charged each other. Below them, the Pokémon and their clones kept fighting ...

Ash couldn't stand seeing the Pokémon get hurt. So he ran between **Mew** and **Mewtwo** and was knocked out!

All of the Pokémon felt bad for Ash. They cried, and their tears revived him. When **Mewtwo** saw this, it realized that humans and Pokémon could live in peace. It ended the battle.

So the battle between **Mew** and **Mewtwo** ended in a tie. But the argument between their fans lives on!

Standing Up to Psychic Trainers

If you are training to be a Pokémon Master, you will have to battle Gym Leaders. Some of those Gym Leaders will be experts in Psychic Pokémon. Here are some Psychic Type experts you may meet on your journey.

Gym Leader: Sabrina
Where: Saffron City, Kanto region
Pokémon: Kadabra, Mr. Mime, Venomoth, Alakazam
Reward: Marsh Badge

What You Need to Know: Creepy Sabrina tries to psych out the Trainers who face her. Don't let her get to you. And be sure to have a strong Ghost Pokémon on your team so you can beat her!

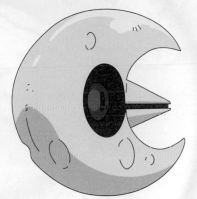

Gym Leaders: Tate and Liza

Where: Mossdeep City, Hoenn region
Pokémon: **Lunatone**, **Solrock**
Reward: Mind Badge

What You Need to Know: Tate and Liza are brother and sister, and they battle together. The two Gym Leaders live in Mossdeep City, which is home to a Space Center. The Mossdeep Gym is designed to look like outer space!

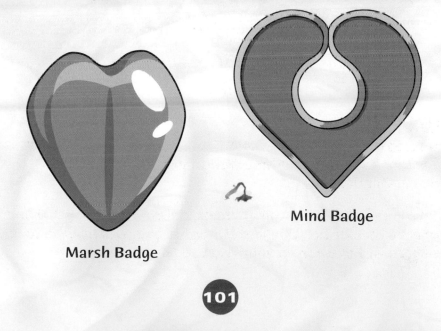

Marsh Badge

Mind Badge

Meet James

Everyone knows that James is a member of Team Rocket. He started out life as a rich boy. Then when his parents wanted to force him to get married, he left home. James didn't have any skills to get a job, so he ended up joining Team Rocket instead! We talked to James about his Pokémon.

James, we always thought you liked Poison Pokémon best.
*I do like Poison Pokémon. They are so effective in battle! My **Weezing** and **Victreebel** never let me down.*

But we heard that Chimecho is your new favorite. And Chimecho is a Psychic Pokémon.
*Oh, my sweet little **Chimecho**! I saw one at a fair once when I was a little boy. I always wanted one. I love the way they swing in the breeze.*

So why don't you let your Chimecho battle?
I couldn't do that! It might get hurt! What if Ash's nasty **Pikachu** zapped it with Thundershock? I couldn't stand it.

By the way, why do you keep trying to catch Pikachu? You haven't succeeded yet.
Team Rocket never gives up! Besides, we have nothing better to do.

We bet Jessie wouldn't want to hear you say that.
You're right! Please don't tell her. She has a pretty mean kick!

Don't worry, James. We won't tell her. Thanks for talking to us!
Looks like I'm blasting off again!

So Long!

You have just seen into the future . . . and it's filled with Psychic Pokémon! Your head is probably spinning from all of the mind-bending feats you have read about. That's okay. You are safe here.

It takes a strong Trainer to handle Psychic Pokémon—a Trainer who won't give up. But if you devote yourself to becoming a Psychic Pokémon Master, the rewards are great. Just think what your friends will say if you catch **Mewtwo**!

Make sure that you check out www.Pokemon.com for more tips on caring for your Psychic Pokémon. We predict that you will have lots of fun there!

Indexes

Normal index

Psychic Index

Look for other

books from
Scholastic